*CPD guide to*

# Roles & Responsibilities of Directors

## Richard Winfield
improving board performance

Brefi Press
www.brefipress.com

First published in 2016 by Brefi Press

ISBN 978-0-948537-38-7

www.brefipress.com

# The Director Development Centre

*This is what we stand for...*

## Our Vision
Boards of directors providing strategic, moral and ethical leadership to transform the world's economy.

## Mission Statement
"We help directors and boards be more effective in clarifying goals, improving communication and applying good corporate governance."

*So, how can we help you?*

## CPD for Directors
Monthly professional development programme delivered by post:

- A4 CPD Record journal (annual)
- 48+ page CPD Guides
- CD audios with interview
- *Directors Briefing* newsletters with legal and regulatory updates, news stories and case studies.

## The Essential Directorship Masterclass
- Multi-media self study programme
- Comprehensive full colour workbook
- 30+ videos (online streaming)

## The New Directors Handbook
- 170 pages covering directors, boards, compliance and strategy
- Download your FREE copy of the first three chapters at:
  www.newdirectors.info

## On-line programmes
- Webinars – occasional series covering specific issues
- Tutorial groups – private membership groups with tuition, discussion and Q&A

## Live workshops
- Induction days – all you need to know for your first 100 days
- Mastermind groups - a mix of focused teaching and peer to peer support

**Find out more:**
**www.CorporateDirector.co.uk**

# Books by Richard Winfield

The New Directors Handbook

The AIM Directors Handbook

Essential Checklists for Directors and Boards

Reflections of a Corporate Coach

Stories from a Corporate Coach

Lessons from a Corporate Coach – Coaching

Lessons from a Corporate Coach – Business

www.brefipress.com

# Contents

# 1. Role of the board of directors

The board's key purpose is to ensure the company's prosperity by collectively directing the company's affairs, whilst meeting the appropriate interests of its shareholders and stakeholders.

The board of directors is responsible for:

- Compliance

- Strategy

How the company is to operate is laid out in the Articles of Association. Every director should obtain a copy of the company's Articles and read, mark, and understand these rules.

According to the UK Institute of Directors, the tasks of the board are as follows:

## Establish vision, mission and values

- Determine the company's vision and mission to guide and set the pace for its current operations and future development.

- Determine the values to be promoted throughout the company.

- Determine and review company goals.

- Determine company policies.

1

# Set strategy and structure

- Review and evaluate present and future opportunities, threats and risks in the external environment and current and future strengths, weaknesses and risks relating to the company.

- Determine strategic options, select those to be pursued, and decide the means to implement and support them.

- Determine the business strategies and plans that underpin the corporate strategy.

- Ensure that the company's organisational structure and capability are appropriate for implementing the chosen strategies.

# Delegate to management

- Delegate authority to management, and monitor and evaluate the implementation of policies, strategies and business plans.

- Determine monitoring criteria to be used by the board.

- Ensure that internal controls are effective.

- Communicate with senior management.

## Exercise accountability to shareholders and be responsible to relevant stakeholders

- Ensure that communications both to and from shareholders and relevant stakeholders are effective.

- Understand and take into account the interests of shareholders and relevant stakeholders.

- Monitor relations with shareholders and relevant stakeholders by gathering and evaluation of appropriate information.

- Promote the goodwill and support of shareholders and relevant stakeholders.

*CPD guide to*

# 2. Responsibilities of directors

Directors are appointed by the shareholders to look after the affairs of the company, and are in a position of trust. This raises the possibility of them abusing their position in order to profit at the expense of their company, and, therefore, at the expense of the shareholders of the company.

Consequently, the law imposes a number of duties, burdens and responsibilities upon directors to prevent abuse. Much of company law can be seen as a balance between allowing directors to manage the company's business so as to make a profit, and preventing them from abusing this freedom.

Directors are responsible for ensuring that proper books of account are kept.

Even though a company is a separate legal person, there are circumstances in which a director can be required to help pay its debts. For example, directors of a company who try to 'trade out of difficulty' and fail may be found guilty of 'wrongful trading' and can be made personally liable. Directors are particularly vulnerable if they have acted in a way that benefits themselves.

- The directors must always exercise their powers for a 'proper purpose' – that is, in furtherance of the reason for which they were given those powers by the shareholders.

- Directors must act in good faith in what they honestly believe to be the best interests of the company, and not for any collateral purpose. This means that, particularly in the event of a conflict of interest between the company's interests and their own, the directors must always favour the company.

- Directors must act with due skill and care.

- Directors must consider the interests of employees of the company.

## Calling a directors' meeting

A director, or the secretary at the request of a director, may call a directors' meeting. A secretary may not call a meeting unless requested to do so by a director or the directors. Each director must be given reasonable notice of the meeting, stating its date, time and place. Commonly, seven days is given but what is 'reasonable' depends in the last resort on the circumstances.

# 3. UK Companies Act 2006

The Companies Act, sections 170-178, sets out the legal responsibilities and general duties of company directors in the Statement of General Duties of Directors. The Act is based on established common law principles and case law, but also includes important reforms which affect all directors – executive or non-executive – in companies of every size.

In particular, it introduced the concept of 'enlightened shareholder value'. Previously, directors focused solely on shareholders' interests; enlightened stakeholder value means taking account of other stakeholders as well.

The Act introduced a code of Directors' Duties, which applies to all companies. Here is a summary of the main principles prepared by the Association of Chartered Certified Accountants.

**The general duties** mean a director must act in the interests of the company and not in the interests of any other parties – including shareholders. This applies even for 'one man' companies, which means a sole shareholder or director may not put their interests above that of the company.

## Duty to act within the company's powers

In addition to the duties and responsibilities imposed on directors by the Act, every company will have its own set of rules known as its 'constitution'.

- Directors must act in accordance with the company's constitution, and only exercise powers for the purposes for which they are conferred.

- They must use the powers designated to them by the shareholders for the benefit of the company.

## Duty to promote the success of the company

The term 'success' is not defined in the Act because this may vary from company to company. In most cases, however, it is likely to mean sustainable profitability. The underlying principle here is that every director has a legal duty to try and act in such a way which, in their judgement, is most likely to bring 'success' to the company.

**Duty to promote the success of the company**

The term 'success' is not defined in the Act because this may vary from company to company. In most cases, however, it is likely to mean sustainable profitability. The underlying principle here is that every director has a legal duty to try and act in such a way which, in their judgement, is most likely to bring 'success' to the company.

As part of its decision making process, a board must act in the way it considers, in good faith, would be most likely to promote the success of the company for the benefit of its members as a whole, and in doing so have regard (amongst other matters) to:

- the likely consequences of any decision in the long term

- the interests of the company's employees

- the need to foster the company's business relationships with suppliers, customers and others

- the impact of the company's operations on the community and the environment

- the desirability of the company maintaining a reputation for high standards of business conduct

- the need to act fairly as between members of the company.

## Duty to exercise independent judgement

This is self explanatory but the Act will not be breached if you exercise your duties in line with any prior agreement with the company or with the company's constitution.

## Duty of skill, care and diligence

Every director must exercise reasonable care, skill and diligence in everything they do for the company. The duty is broken into two parts:

- As a director you must demonstrate the general knowledge and skill reasonably expected of a person carrying out the functions you carry out in relation to the company. Therefore, a managing director will be expected to have a knowledge of all areas of the business or to have engaged people who can help them; and

- As a director you must act in accordance with any specific general knowledge and skills you actually have. Therefore, a director who is a qualified accountant would be expected to show a greater general knowledge, skills and interest in relation to financial aspects of the company than another director who was not so qualified.

## Duty to avoid conflicts of interest

You must avoid any situations where you have any personal or outside interests which will potentially come into conflict with those of the company.

This duty even extends to former directors.

However, this duty is not infringed if:

- the situation cannot reasonably be regarded as likely to give rise to a conflict; or

- the matter has been authorised by the directors, as appropriate to the type of company (public companies must give the directors specific powers in their articles)

## Duty not to accept benefits from third parties

A director of a company must not accept a benefit from a third party arising from them being a director; or from their actions as a director.

Any benefits that cannot reasonably be regarded as likely to give rise to a conflict of interest can be ignored.

This duty also applies to former directors.

# Duty to declare an interest in a proposed transaction or arrangement

The Act states: "If a director of a company is in any way, directly or indirectly, interested in a proposed transaction or arrangement with the company he [she] must declare the nature and extent of that interest to the other directors."

The declaration of an interest can be either verbal or written but must comply with the requirements set out in the Act.

The Act also requires directors to consider a number of factors when making decisions, including the interests of the company's employees and the impact of the company's operations on the community and the environment. The duty only extends to considering the decisions' impact.

*CPD guide to*

# 4. Types of director

The ultimate control as to the composition of the board of directors rests with the shareholders, who can always appoint, and – more importantly, sometimes – dismiss a director. The shareholders can also fix the minimum and maximum number of directors. However, the board can usually appoint (but not dismiss) a director to this office as well. A director may be dismissed from office by a majority vote of the shareholders, provided that a special procedure is followed. The procedure is complex, and legal advice will always be required.

## Chairman

The chairman creates the conditions for overall board and individual director effectiveness. With the help of the executive directors and the company secretary, the chairman sets the agenda for the board's deliberations and ensures that strategy, performance, value creation and accountability, and issues relevant to these areas are reserved for board decision.

It is the responsibility of the chairman to:

- Create a climate in which thought and expression may flourish naturally

- Bring both individual and collective views together in a cohesive form

- Ensure awareness of what has been decided

13

The chairman also ensures effective communication with shareholders and other stakeholders and, in particular, that all directors are made aware of the views of those who provide the company's capital.

The chairman of each board committee fulfils an important leadership role similar to that of the chairman of the board, particularly in creating the conditions for overall committee and individual director effectiveness.

# Executive director

Most executive directors have a management role, but it might be as an internal advisor or specialist.

They have the same duties as other members of the board. These duties extend to the whole of the business, and not just that part of it covered by their individual executive roles.

Executive directors have the most intimate knowledge of the company and its capabilities when developing and presenting proposals, and when exercising judgements, particularly on matters of strategy. They should appreciate that constructive challenge from non-executive directors is an essential aspect of good governance, and should encourage their non-executive colleagues to test their proposal in the light of the non-executives' wider experience outside the company. The chairman and the CEO should ensure that this process is properly followed.

# Non-executive director

Non-executive directors (NEDs) are members of the board of directors without executive responsibilities in the company. Legally speaking, there is no distinction between an executive and a non-executive director; they have the same legal duties, responsibilities and potential liabilities as their executive counterparts. They attend board meetings and contribute to discussions and decision-making.

NEDs are appointed from outside the organisation for their independence, expertise and contacts to bring judgement and experience to the deliberations of the board that the executive directors on their own would lack. Whereas the executive director has an intimate knowledge of the company, the non-executive director may be expected to have a wider perspective of the world at large.

# Senior Independent Director

The boards of publicly listed companies should appoint a senior independent director from among their independent non-executives. To qualify as "independent", non-executives need to have the necessary independence of character and judgement and also be free of any connections that may lead to a conflict of interest. This means not having any contractual or other relationship with the company or its directors apart from the current office of director and not being subject to any control or influence of a third party which could affect the exercise of independent judgement.

Senior independent directors serve as a sounding board for the chairman and act as an intermediary for the other directors. They are responsible for holding annual meetings with non-executives, without the chairman present, to appraise the chairman's performance. They would also be expected to meet with the non-executives on other such occasions when necessary.

When the board is undergoing a period of stress, the senior independent director's role becomes vitally important. He or she is expected to work with the chairman and the other directors, and/or shareholders, to resolve major issues. For example, they can act as an alternative point of contact for investors who may have made little headway in discussions with the chairman, chief executive or finance director – or who may have concerns about the performance of these individuals. Where the relationship between the chairman and chief executive is particularly close, and they do not communicate fully with shareholders, the senior independent director is able to step in and provide a link.

Where there is a disagreement or dispute between the chairman and the chief executive, the senior independent director can intervene, identify issues that have caused the rift and try to mediate and build a consensus.

## Chief Executive (CEO)

The chief executive is the most senior executive director on the board, with responsibility for proposing strategy to the board and for delivering the strategy as agreed. Their role is one of implementation; to implement board policy and report to the board on all aspects of that policy implementation.

They are accountable to the chairman and the board and are responsible for the management of the company within the guidelines laid down by the board, to which the CEO will also contribute.

The chief executive is responsible for devising the most appropriate management structure for the company and for recruiting, managing, motivating and retaining an effective management team, paying due regard to the needs of the future. It is up to them to communicate the company's values and behaviour right through the company.

They should ensure that the board is provided with the reports and information it needs, both to monitor company performance and to take those decisions that are its collective responsibility.

The CEO's relationship with the chairman is a key relationship that can help the board be more effective; the differing responsibilities of the chairman and CEO should be set out in writing and agreed by the board. The CEO is responsible for supporting the chairman to make certain that appropriate standards of governance permeate through all parts of the organisation.

## Company Secretary

In the UK all public companies are obliged to have a company secretary; private companies are no longer required to do so, unless their articles of association explicitly require them to. A company secretary does not need to be an individual but can instead be another company or a partnership.

A company secretary may not be a director, but will attend all board meetings and is directly answerable to the board; one of their prime functions is to produce minutes of a board meeting, which must be kept for at least 10 years.

The secretary will often be liable for breach of duty in the same way as board members. If they have prime responsibility for statutory tasks and there is a failure to comply, they will be the person in default and liable to a fine.

In a public company, the directors must make sure, as far as is reasonably possible, that the secretary has "the requisite knowledge and experience to discharge the functions of secretary of the company" and has the requisite qualifications, such as chartered accountant or chartered secretary.

They are responsible for advising the directors and board, maintaining the company's statutory registers and books, and filing annual returns. They arrange meetings of the company's directors and shareholders and ensure proper notices of meetings are issued; they prepare agendas, circulate relevant papers and take and produce minutes to record the business transacted at the meetings and the decisions taken.

The obligations and responsibilities of the company secretary necessitate them playing a leading role in the good governance of companies by supporting the chairman and helping the board and its committees to function efficiently.

The company secretary should report to the chairman on all board governance matters. This does not preclude them from also reporting to the CEO in relation to his or her other executive management responsibilities.

The appointment and removal of the company secretary should be a matter for the board as a whole, and the remuneration of the company secretary might be determined by the remuneration committee.

## Chief Financial Officer (CFO)

The chief financial officer has a particular responsibility to deliver high quality information to the board on the financial position of the company.

## Nominee director

A nominee director is one who acts as a non-executive director on the board of a company on behalf of another person or firm such as a bank, investor, or lender.

Nominee directors carry the same responsibilities, and risks, as other directors.

Nominee directorships can sometimes be useful, for example in preparing "off-the-shelf" ready-made companies. But the nominee system can be used to disguise control and is open to abuse if the nominee secretly hands back all control to the real owner. In many such cases they are residents of tax havens acting on behalf of non-residents as a trustee on the board of an off-shore firm in that haven.

# De facto director

The UK Companies Act simply defines a director as including any person occupying the position of director, by whatever name called.

A *de facto* director is someone who has not been legally appointed and notified to Companies House as a director but who nevertheless acts as a director and holds them self out to third parties as a director.

The matter is determined on an objective basis and irrespective of the person's motivation or belief. There is no definitive test to determine the issue and all relevant facts need to be taken into account in determining whether or not you will be deemed to be a de-factor director.

It is the role of the individual, rather than the title used that determines whether an individual is a director or not. The *de facto* director will usually carry out all the duties of a director and can make the decisions of a director, sign company documents and be treated as a director by other directors.

The *de facto* director is subject to the same legal duties, responsibilities and potential liabilities as *de jure* directors and will be treated as such by the courts in the case of a dispute.

Relevant factors they will consider include:

- Whether there were other persons acting as directors

- Whether the individual has been held out is acting as a director, including using the title director in

communications, or has been considered to be
director by the company or third parties

• Whether the individual was part of the corporate
governing structure

• In what capacity of the individual was acting

Acts of a de-facto director can include:

• Accepting responsibility for the company's financial
affairs

• Acting as sole signatory for the company bank
account

• Negotiating with third parties on behalf of the board

• In recruiting and appointing senior management
positions

## Shadow director

A shadow director is a person in accordance with whose
directions or instructions the directors of a company are
accustomed to act. Under this definition, it is possible that a
director, or the whole board, of a holding company, and the
holding company itself, could be treated as a shadow
director of a subsidiary.

A founder or significant shareholder who wishes to escape
the disclosure requirements of a directorship might still be
counted as a 'shadow' director and held responsible for
actions as if he or she were a formal director.

Professional advisors giving advice in their professional capacity are specifically excluded from the definition of a shadow director in UK companies legislation.

# 5. Role of the chairman

The company's articles of association usually provide for the election of a chairman of the board. They empower the directors to appoint one of their own number as chairman and to determine the period for which he is to hold office. If no chairman is elected, or the elected chairman is not present within five minutes of the time fixed for a directors' meeting or is unwilling to preside, those directors in attendance may usually elect one of their number as chairman of the meeting.

Since the chairman's position is of great importance, it is vital that his/her election is clearly in accordance with any special procedure laid down by the articles and that it is unambiguously minuted; this is especially important to avoid disputes as to his/her period in office. Usually there is no special procedure for resignation. As for removal, articles usually empower the board to remove the chairman from office at any time. Proper and clear minutes are important in order to avoid disputes.

The chairman's role is pivotal to the operation of the board. He or she must coordinate the contributions of the non-executive directors to ensure that the executive team is subject to a sufficient degree of oversight.

As a general rule, the chief executive leads the management team and runs the company while the chairman leads the board. The chairman must be sufficiently informed, engaged and able to intervene when required, but must avoid becoming too involved with the day-to-day business of the company. Board dysfunction is likely to result when the distinct roles of the chief executive and chairman are not properly understood or respected.

The chairman's role includes managing the board's business and acting as its facilitator and guide. This can include:

- Determining board composition and organisation;

- Clarifying board and management responsibilities;

- Planning and managing board and board committee meetings;

- Developing the effectiveness of the board.

The company's articles might give the chairman a second, 'casting', vote to be used in the case of equality of votes. However, a chairman does not have a casting vote merely by virtue of his office.

# What makes an outstanding chairman?

A study by INSEAD identified three characteristics of good chairmen: personal humility, listening, while challenging and supporting the board and the 'guts' to do what is right for the company.

The Directorbank Group surveyed 430 chairmen and directors to discover what makes an outstanding chairman. Here is what they found:

| What makes them outstanding | What causes them to underperform |
|---|---|
| • Charismatic personality with gravitas | • Too partisan, not impartial |
| • Good communicator and listener | • Poor leadership |
| • Clear sense of direction | • Too aloof and not involved |
| • Strategic view – the big picture | • Arrogant, over-opinionated and domineering |
| • Allows CEO to get on with their job | • Poor control of the board |
| • Good at governance; managing meetings | • Unable to make difficult decisions |
| • Public presence | • Doesn't properly understand the business |
| • Broad experience | • Poor sector knowledge |
| • Network of contacts | • Poor communicator |
| • Business acumen; understands the business | |
| • Able to bring people together | |
| • A mentor and coach; offers support and advice | |
| • Able to gain shareholders' confidence | |
| • Able to get to the key issue quickly | |

# 6. The non-executive director

Non-executive directors are appointed to monitor executive activity and contribute to the development of strategy. This is a complex and demanding role that requires skills, experience, integrity and particular behaviours and personal attributes and it is the responsibility of the chairman to create accountability between the executives and non-executives.

In small companies they can contribute corporate expertise and provide a mentoring role. In larger companies an appointment can provide a training opportunity as a first experience on a board.

Non-executive directors need to be sound in judgement and to have an enquiring mind. They should question intelligently, debate constructively, challenge rigorously and decide dispassionately; and they should listen sensitively to the views of others, inside and outside the board.

A function of NEDs is to improve the quality of decision-making by the board by: bringing a range of skills and experience to the deliberations of the board; acting as a counterbalance, where necessary, to the influence of the chairman or CEO over board decision-making. They can make an important contribution to strategy by noticing blind spots and challenging executives to think laterally about options, alternatives and aspirations in a way that is nevertheless felt to be supportive. It is the combination of informed challenge and support that executives most desire and value in the contribution of non-executives.

The key to non-executive effectiveness lies not in strengthening either the control or strategic aspects of their role but in the strength and rigour of the process of accountability that they establish and maintain in their relationships with executives; accountability that spans issues of both their direction and control of the company.

In contrast to executives, non-executive directors are normally remunerated on a fixed-fee basis. This is to ensure that non-executives retain an objective and independent perspective on the activities of the company. For this reason, share options would not normally form part of a non-executive's remuneration framework.

Acting as an NED on the board of a young company that is dominated by the founder(s) and owners can require particularly sensitive soft skills of rapport building and communication, as well as decision making, vision and imagination. However, an NED with experience in larger or more established organisations can play a significant, if unacknowledged, role as a mentor in smaller ones.

To be effective, a non-executive director has to understand the company's business, but the experience and qualities required of an NED can be obtained from working in other industries or in other aspects of commercial and public life. NEDs might, therefore, include individuals who:

- are executive directors in other public companies;

- hold NED positions and chairmanship positions in other public companies;

- have professional qualifications (e.g. partners in firms of solicitors);

- have experience in government, as politicians or former senior civil servants.

The Higgs Report, 2003, looked at the role and effectiveness of NEDs, and many of the Higgs recommendations are now included in the UK Corporate Governance Code.

The Higgs *Suggestions for Good Practice* states that the role of a NED has several key elements, which non-executives are perhaps in a better position to provide than executives. These are:

- **Strategy:** NEDs should constructively challenge and help to develop proposals on strategy.

- **Performance:** NEDs should scrutinise the performance of executive management in achieving agreed goals and objectives, and monitor the reporting of performance.

- **Risk:** NEDs should satisfy themselves about the integrity of financial information and that the systems of internal controls and risk management are robust.

- **People:** NEDs are responsible for deciding the level of remuneration for executive directors, and should have a prime role in appointing directors (and removing them where necessary) and in succession planning.

These roles explain the requirements for audit, remuneration and nomination committees consisting of independent non-executive directors.

Much of their effectiveness depends on exercising influence rather than giving orders and requires the establishment of a spirit of partnership and mutual respect across the board. Non-executive directors need to build recognition by executives of their contribution in order to promote openness and trust. Only then can they contribute effectively. The key to non-executive effectiveness lies as much in behaviours and relationships as in structures and processes.

# Independence of non-executive directors

The independence of a non-executive director could be challenged, for example, if the individual concerned:

- has a family connection with the CEO – a problem in some family-controlled public companies;

- until recently used to be an executive director in the company;

- until recently used to work for the company in a professional capacity (e.g. as its auditor or corporate lawyer);

- receives payments from the company in addition to their fees as an NED.

A key principle of good corporate governance is that there should be a sufficient number of independent NEDs on the board to create a suitable balance of power and prevent the dominance of the board by one individual or a small number of individuals.

A person cannot be independent if he or she personally stands to gain or otherwise benefit substantially from:

- income from the company, in addition to his or her fee as a NED;

- the company's reported profitability and movements in the company's share price.

These criteria of independence should be applied to a chairman as well as other non-executive directors.

# Case study

The Kazhakstan mining company Kazakhmys attracted attention by becoming a listed UK company in October 2005 and a member of the FTSE 100. Although the company took steps to strengthen its corporate governance, its practices still fell short of normal UK listed company practice. Its chairman was not independent and there were doubts about the independence of the NEDs in view of the requirement of the Combined Code that independence means being free from relationships that affect, or could appear to affect, the judgement of the director.

One NED was a director of a company that had a large secured interest-free loan from Kazakhmys. Another NED received payment for services to the company in relation to its London listing. A third NED was vice chairman of investment banking at J P Morgan Cazenove, financial advisers to Kazakhmys.

A more general debate arose as a result of this case around whether corporate governance standards in the UK would come under threat as more foreign companies join the London market. Index-tracking funds would have to buy shares in these companies, even if their corporate governance regimes were not up to Corporate Governance Code standards.

# Non-executive directors in small and mid-size quoted companies

According to a report of the triennial Quoted Companies Alliance/BDO Small and Mid-cap Sentiment Index for 2014, boards of small and mid-size quoted companies are relatively happy with the work that their non-executive directors do.

NEDs were seen as trusted members of their teams and clearly provide a unique viewpoint that is highly valued.

83 per cent of respondents felt that they got good value for money from their NEDs. They valued most their broader business experience, the fact that they provide checks and balances and the improvements in governance that they can bring to a company.

Non-executive directors in such companies work on average 14 hours per month and hold approximately three non-executive director roles. On average, they were paid £33,400 a year per role.

The report recommended that companies should do more to let their NEDs know what is expected of them. Demonstrating the valuable contribution of the NEDs on a board is an important way to inspire the confidence of private investors.

# David Jones' recommendations for non-executive directors

David Jones was chief executive of the clothing retailer NEXT from 1988 until 2001 before becoming its chairman. In his business autobiography, *Next to Me*, he makes six recommendations for a new code of corporate governance with respect to non-executive directors:

- First, change the title of non-executive directors to 'independent directors', and call executive directors 'operating directors'. Independence of mind and a degree of distance from the internal politics and pressures of the day-to-day operations of the company are the key requirements. They are expected to be independent, so why not call them that?

- Second, make the senior independent director the deputy chairman, to ensure that his or her authority is clear to everyone, internally and externally.

- Third, ensure that there are an equal number of independent and operating directors. Balance is essential, and it is up to a skilled chairman to find

33

consensus or exercise judgment if there is disagreement between the two groups.

- Fourth, insist that the independent directors spend at least three days of every month in the business. They must have a good knowledge of how the business operates in order to make a worthwhile contribution at board meetings. There is no excuse for not knowing what the executive directors are talking about or not understanding the board report. In addition, they must know the second tier of management to satisfy themselves that there is indeed a viable succession plan.

- Fifth, for the same reasons no-one – however, wise or well connected they may be – should be permitted to have more than three public independent directorships.

- Sixth, make it mandatory that the annual accounts of every public limited company should include a signed statement from each independent director confirming that they have had access to all the relevant information to enable them to do their jobs efficiently.

# 7. Building a better board

Although the formal authority to elect directors lies with the shareholders, the power to nominate board members is the key to forming an effective board.

Building an effective board takes time and patience on the part of board members, and benefits from a professional approach to boardroom procedure.

Highly effective boards include a mix of directors with expertise and experience to fulfil their essential oversight roles. Having a board made up of the right people with the relevant skill sets is critical in today's competitive business environment.

The chairman has a particular responsibility in welding a group of capable individuals into an effective board team. The chairman has to find a way to reach a consensus between diverging views on the company and its future. An atmosphere of open discussion should be encouraged. Perspectives and viewpoints should be properly documented in the minutes, allowing dissenting voices to be recorded. There should also be a clear formulation of decisions, so that the decision-making process is followed by decisive action.

## Minimum skills

A board must have the minimum skills required to adequately cover the unique issues, risks and challenges that the particular business faces and these skills must be up to date.

In their book *Board Composition and Corporate Performance* (2003), Keil and Nicholson describe a high performing board as having:

- Leaders

- Visionaries or strategic thinkers

- Practical people

- Analytical people

- Communicators who can deal with stakeholder groups.

Not all directors will possess each necessary skill but the board as a whole must possess them, and each member of the board must be able to work with the group in a constructive way that ensures there is a rigorous debate whilst remaining a highly functional group.

## Diversity

Diversity adds great value to boards, whether by way of gender diversity or broader ethnic, cultural, age, or socioeconomic diversity. The advantage of different viewpoints from directors of different backgrounds can often lead to a broader understanding of a particular issue and in doing so a more measured outcome.

## Practical tips

Juliet de Baubigny, a senior partner at Kleiner Perkins Caufield & Byers has identified some practical tips to help CEOs assemble a great board.

**Know the company's vision.** Where do you want the company to go? Define what you need the board to do to achieve those goals. Keep that in mind as you consider and define the attributes, skills, and experiences that you need of your board members.

**Seek the right skills.** Create a simple grid combining attributes that actually exist in the market. Draft a table with all the desired aspects of a "final" board. Fill in the table with prospective ideas for each director, ranking each in terms of depth or fit and whether that person can be recruited. Keep this list current, fresh, and ongoing, and make it an active item of discussion at board meetings.

**Develop roles and responsibilities for members.** As Jim Collins says, "Do you have the right people in the right seats on the bus?" It's never too early to have committees or key areas of responsibility. Do you have the best head of audit, compensation etc.? Who are the lead directors that you as CEO can rely on in each critical area?

**Build a culture and invite debate.** Foster a culture of open feedback and independence. You want different opinions and perspectives to help you consider alternatives. Consider the culture and interaction you want from your board: passionate and intense debate, or cerebral and deliberative? You want to recruit a board that pushes you, makes you uncomfortable and challenges conventional wisdom. At the same time, you want a board and not an operating committee – so setting boundaries is important.

**Break through your comfort zone.** Boards tend to reach for what's familiar and comfortable, which results in homogeneity. Knowing that, you should strive for diversity of opinion and not be afraid to go against the grain. Keeping that top of mind will help you be open-minded to alternatives you would not have considered in the first place.

Board building is an ongoing activity, a process of continuous improvement, which means boards must keep coming back to the same questions about purpose, resources, and effectiveness. The best mechanisms for doing that are annual self-assessments. According to a survey undertaken by Mercer Delta Consulting and reported in the *Harvard Business Review* (May 2004), conducting and acting on such assessments are among the top activities most likely to improve board performance overall.

# Board types

Boards must decide how engaged they want to be in influencing management's decisions and the company's direction. Mercer Delta Consulting have identified five board types that fall along a continuum from least to most involved. They recommend that at the start of any board-building programme, the directors and the CEO should agree among themselves which of the following models best fits the company.

## The Passive Board

This is the traditional model. The board's activity and participation are minimal and at the CEO's discretion. The board has limited accountability. Its main job is ratifying management's decisions.

# The Certifying Board

This model emphasises credibility to shareholders and the importance of outside directors. The board certifies that the business is managed properly and that the CEO meets the board's requirements. It also oversees an orderly succession process.

# The Engaged Board

In this model, the board serves as the CEO's partner. It provides insight, advice, and support on key decisions. It recognises its responsibility for overseeing CEO and company performance. The board conducts substantive discussions of key issues and actively defines its role and boundaries.

# The Intervening Board

This model is common in a crisis. The board becomes deeply involved in making key decisions about the company and holds frequent, intense meetings.

# The Operating Board

This is the deepest level of ongoing board involvement. The board makes key decisions that management then implements. This model is common in early-stage start-ups whose top executives may have specialised expertise but lack broad management experience.

Establishing an overarching level of engagement helps board directors set expectations and ground rules for their roles relative to senior managers' roles. But an engagement philosophy – like most expressions of general principle –

does not apply equally to all spheres of activity. Boards, after all, potentially participate in dozens of distinct areas.

# Balancing a board with personality and skills

The essential step in building a first class professional board is to relate it to the company's needs. Every board should have a rationale – that is there should be an essential logic behind its size, structure and specific membership.

It is important to ensure that due care is taken over the choice of board members, and that board members have the necessary skills and competencies to fulfil their responsibilities. Executive directors will need to undertake specialised professional training if they are to effectively make the transition from operational manager (with a focus on one aspect of a firm's activities) to company director (where they must exercise oversight over the firm as a whole).

A board must gel as a team and, as a team, control management. Any behaviour gap – undue influence, reliance, dislike, dysfunction or even contempt – by one or more directors or managers, introduces information and oversight asymmetry that can lead to governance failure.

Good boards have competency, diversity and behaviour matrices and performance reviews that define and rate behaviours at the board table, have peer reviews and mentoring that develops and refines behaviours, and act on the results regardless of profile or tenure.

In the Hermes *Responsible Capitalism Survey*, 2014, over 85% of institutional investors identified having a range of diverse professional experiences at board level and an independent board as important corporate governance practices when looking to make an investment.

The Australian Institute of Directors believes that two main sets of criteria should be met in determining the competencies required in a director:

- Behavioural attributes that contribute to an effective group dynamic. Each board member needs to be able to work with the group in a constructive way that ensures there is rigorous debate whilst remaining a highly functioning group.

- A board must have the minimum skills required to adequately cover the unique issues, risks and challenges that the particular business faces and these skills must be up to date.

Individual directors and the board overall must make efforts to ensure each member remains up to date in both skills and knowledge.

The board must make an effort to regularly measure and assess the contribution each board member makes and take steps to address any deficiencies that become apparent. It should regularly audit the skills required by the company and adapt or make changes to the board membership according to changing needs.

Evaluation of directors should be undertaken by the nominating committee and its independent advisor, not by management.

Competencies for board members can be broken into job-related skills necessary to do their job and personal qualities:

## Job-related competencies

- Strategic expertise – the ability to review the strategy through constructive questioning and suggestion.

- Accounting and finance – the ability to read and comprehend the company's accounts, financial material presented to the board, financial reporting requirements and some understanding of corporate finance.

- Legal – the board's responsibility involves overseeing compliance with numerous laws as well as understanding an individual director's legal duties and responsibilities.

- Managing risk – experience in managing areas of major risk to the organisation.

- Managing people and achieving change.

- Experience with financial markets.

- Industry knowledge – experience in similar organisations or industries.

## Personal qualities

- An effective and persuasive communicator whose contribution is concise, objective and clear.

- Socially competent with a deft touch of humour.

- Independent of mind without prejudicing loyalty to colleagues and the board.

- A good listener who can focus on key issues and respond with sound advice.

- Democratic in balancing the interests of shareholders against the interests of others involved in the business.

- An achiever in his or her own particular chosen field.

- Constructive in expressing ideas as an individual when divorced from the structure and props of his or her own organisation (non-executive directors)

- Positive in making statements and proposals, and unwilling to acquiesce in silence.

# Personality profiling

Personality profiling is a means of studying the dynamic structure of a team and matching individuals to roles and responsibilities.

Individual and team profile analysis is a systematic procedure designed to measure personal behavioural styles. Profiling helps individuals gain an understanding of their working style, how this impacts on their relationships with others in the business environment, and how they might develop to improve their effectiveness both as a person and as a professional.  It enables them to further enhance their inter-personal skills, improving team performance and creating a more positive, productive cultural environment.

Although it is very useful for individuals to understand both how they operate and where best to target their talents, the real benefit is when a whole team can be profiled and then discuss how the team works together.

Profiling systems include DISC, Belbin Team Roles and Myers-Briggs Type Indicator. Brefi Group uses the Wealth Dynamics system.

## Wealth Dynamics

Wealth Dynamics is a very user-friendly profiling system that defines eight profiles in terms of the roles in which different individuals are most likely to be successful.  This will identify strengths and weaknesses in the balance of the board, which, when related to the experience/knowledge/skills register, can be used in future recruitment.

The same model can also be used to understand individual business cycles, markets and international economies.

You can learn about Wealth Dynamics and obtain a personal profile at: www.knowyourprofile.com.

An on-line system provides individual printed reports. However, it is desirable for both the individual and the team to receive an explanation of the system and personal feedback from a qualified consultant.

# 8. Succession planning and recruitment

Appointing directors who are able to make a positive contribution is one of the key elements of board effectiveness. Directors will be more likely to make good decisions and maximise the opportunities for the company's success in the longer term if the right skill sets are present in the boardroom. This includes the appropriate range and balance of skills, experience, knowledge and independence. Non-executive directors should possess critical skills of value to the board and relevant to the challenges facing the company.

Given the importance of committees in many companies' decision-making structures, it will be important to recruit non-executives with the necessary technical skills and knowledge relating to the committees' subject matter, as well as the potential to assume the role of committee chairman.

For an organisation to plan for the replacement of key managers and directors from within, potential candidates must first be identified and prepared to take on those roles.

Succession planning is a means for an organisation to ensure its continued effective performance through leadership continuity. When recruiting new directors it is important to be clear what competencies, skills and experiences are needed on the board and which ones, if any, are missing. To assist in clarifying this information the board should ensure that there is an up-to-date director competency matrix. The process of developing the matrix should describe the competencies, skills, and experiences of the current directors and the key ones required for new directors.

The key steps in the competency matrix development process are likely to be as follows:

- Assess what competencies the board *needs* given the challenges faced by the business and taking into account the strengths and weaknesses of the executive team. The roles and responsibilities of board and management are different but the capabilities of each need to be complementary. Consideration should also be given to weighting particular competencies.

- Assess what competencies each *existing* director possesses. This is done by asking current board members to self assess themselves and their colleagues relative to the matrix. Those self assessments should be reviewed by, for example, the board chair or the nominating committee as some directors tend to be excessively modest while others overestimate themselves.

- Evaluate the extent of any competency gaps resulting from a comparison between steps 1 and 2.

- Define a 'recruitment specification' for the competencies a new director would need to bring to the board to fill defined competency gaps.

This allows potential internal candidates to be "groomed," trained, and mentored for the possibility of filling the leadership positions.

In order to prepare potential directors, the gap between what they are ready for now and what preparation they need to be ready for the job when it is available needs to be determined. This information can help determine what training, experience, and mentoring is needed.

Once the potential directors have been identified, a plan for each of them should be developed. Each potential director should be assigned a mentor; this mentor could be the person whom they might replace.

When the time comes for the position to be filled, there will be several people within the organisation from which to choose, all of whom have had the time to develop for the new role. At least one of them may be ready to meet the requirements.

For non-executive directors and external candidates for senior management roles the same approach should be taken to developing a recruitment specification. This will guide formal searches and form the basis for nomination committees to evaluate candidates. They must then conduct due diligence and closely scrutinise whether individual candidates possess the requisite skill set and qualities to serve on the board.

*CPD guide to*

# 9. Appointing a director

Appointing directors who are able to make a positive contribution is one of the key elements of board effectiveness.

The nomination committee, usually led by the chairman, should be responsible for board recruitment. The process should be continuous and proactive, and should take into account the company's agreed strategic priorities. The aim should be to secure a board which achieves the right balance between challenge and teamwork, and fresh input and thinking, while maintaining a cohesive board.

The chairman's vision for achieving the optimal board composition will help the nomination committee review the skills required, identify gaps, develop transparent appointment criteria and inform succession planning.

It is important to consider a variety of personal attributes among board candidates, including: intellect, critical assessment and judgement, courage, openness, honesty and tact; and the ability to listen, forge relationships and develop trust. Diversity of psychological type, background and gender is important to ensure that a board is not composed solely of like-minded individuals.

Executive directors may be recruited from external sources, but companies should also develop internal talent and capability.

Given the importance of committees in many companies' decision-making structures, it will be important to recruit non-executives with the necessary skills and knowledge relating to the committees' subject matter, as well as the potential to assume the role of committee chairman.

# Terms of engagement

If a prospective non-executive director decides to accept the offer of the appointment, terms of engagement should be agreed with the company (either the board as a whole or its nomination committee).

The terms that must be agreed are as follows:

- The initial period of tenure in office (normally three years);

- Time commitment: the company must indicate how much time the non-executive director is expected to commit to the company, and the non-executive director should make this commitment. This should be included in the formal letter of appointment. This is particularly important in the case of chairmanships;

- Remuneration: the annual remuneration of the non-executive director should be agreed. This may be a fixed annual fee. It is generally considered inappropriate for non-executive directors, including the chairman, to be remunerated on the basis of incentive schemes linked to company performance, because this could undermine their independence.

The terms of engagement should be set out in a formal letter of appointment. As well as including details of the role that the NED will be required to perform (including initial membership of board committees), the expected time commitment, the tenure and the remuneration, the letter of engagement should also:

- specify that the non-executive director should treat all information received as a director as confidential to the company;

- indicate the arrangements for induction;

- give details of directors' and officers' liability insurance that will be available;

- indicate the need for an annual performance review process for directors;

- state what company resources will be made available to the non-executive director.

# The Director Development Centre

*This is what we stand for...*

## Our Vision
Boards of directors providing strategic, moral and ethical leadership to transform the world's economy.

## Mission Statement
"We help directors and boards be more effective in clarifying goals, improving communication and applying good corporate governance."

*So, how can we help you?*

## CPD for Directors
Monthly professional development programme delivered by post:

- A4 CPD Record journal (annual)
- 48+ page CPD Guides
- CD audios with interview
- *Directors Briefing* newsletters with legal and regulatory updates, news stories and case studies.

## The Essential Directorship Masterclass

- Multi-media self study programme
- Comprehensive full colour workbook
- 30+ videos (online streaming)

## The New Directors Handbook
- 170 pages covering directors, boards, compliance and strategy
- Download your FREE copy of the first three chapters at: www.newdirectors.info

## On-line programmes
- Webinars – occasional series covering specific issues
- Tutorial groups – private membership groups with tuition, discussion and Q&A

## Live workshops
- Induction days – all you need to know for your first 100 days
- Mastermind groups - a mix of focused teaching and peer to peer support

**Find out more:**
**www.CorporateDirector.co.uk**

9 780948 537387